This journal belongs to

_____

DATE

_____

THIRTY DAYS TO PEACE

All Scripture quotations, unless otherwise indicated, are taken from the Holy Bible, English Standard Version, ESV® Text Edition® (2016), copyright © 2001 by Crossway Bibles, a publishing ministry of Good News Publishers. All rights reserved. Scripture quotations marked (NIV) are taken from the Holy Bible, New International Version®, NIV®. Copyright © 1973, 1978, 1984 by Biblica Inc.® Used by permission. All rights reserved worldwide.

Trade Paperback ISBN 978-0-7352-9083-9

Copyright © 2017 by WaterBrook

Cover design by Kristopher Orr; cover image and interior illustrations by Laura Elizabeth Marshall

Published in the United States by WaterBrook, an imprint of the Crown Publishing Group, a division of Penguin Random House LLC, New York.

WaterBrook® and its deer colophon are registered trademarks of Penguin Random House LLC.

Printed in China
2017—First Edition

10 9 8 7 6 5 4 3 2 1

SPECIAL SALES
Most WaterBrook books are available at special quantity discounts when purchased in bulk by corporations, organizations, and special-interest groups. Custom imprinting or excerpting can also be done to fit special needs. For information, please e-mail specialmarketscms@penguinrandomhouse.com or call 1-800-603-7051.

30 DAYS TO Peace

A ONE-MONTH CREATIVE JOURNAL

30 DAYS TO Peace

WATERBROOK

Discovering Peace

In our busy and loud lives, it's easy to get sucked into the pandemonium and ignore the life-giving breeze of peace. That's what this journal is for. It's about stopping for a few minutes each day to breathe in and reflect on stillness and harmony.

Although the pages that follow will help you discover what peace means to you, don't overthink the entries. Just respond with your heart. While there are a few questions that will specifically direct you to write, draw, or doodle, feel free to engage with this journal however you prefer—maybe you'd rather paint or collage or include photographs. There are no wrong answers or methods here—all that matters is that you're exploring peace each day!

You'll notice two pages at the end of this journal to write down songs that speak to you during your journey. Once you've written out your full playlist, share it. Create it on Spotify and tweet it to @WaterBrookPress using the hashtag #PlaylistPeace.

Ready to begin?

Turn away
from evil
and do good;

seek peace and pursue it.

PSALM 34:14

How do you define peace?

Seek peace and pursue it.

Peace is not merely

a distant goal

that we seek, but a

means by which we

arrive at that goal.

MARTIN LUTHER KING JR.

Peace can be found in the most mundane tasks.
How can you make something you do every
day a practice in peacefulness?

Mercy,
peace and
love be
yours in
abundance.

JUDE 1:2, NIV

Fill these two pages with colors
that bring to mind peace.

For you shall go out in joy and be led forth in peace; the mountains and the hills before you shall break forth into singing, and all the trees of the field shall clap their hands.

ISAIAH 55:12

Stand outside in creation and take in
everything around you. What is one thing
you encounter that brings you peace?

If God be our God, He will give us peace in trouble. When there is a storm without, He will make peace within. The world can create trouble in peace, but God can create peace in trouble.

THOMAS WATSON

The need to have control is the quickest
way to stop us from finding peace.
What things are you thankful to not have
to control, whether huge or small?

Peace does not dwell in outward things, but in the *heart* prepared to wait *trustfully* and *quietly* on *Him* who has *all* things *safely* in *His* hands.

ELISABETH
ELLIOT

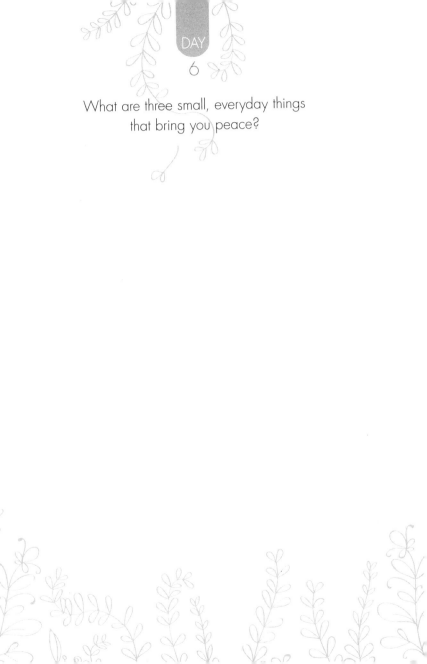

DAY

6

What are three small, everyday things
that bring you peace?

*While you are
proclaiming peace
with your lips,
be careful to have it
even more fully
in your heart.*

ST. FRANCIS
OF ASSISI

Use these two pages to describe
or illustrate peacefulness.

*If possible,
so far as it
depends on you,
live peaceably
with all.*

ROMANS 12:18

Why do you think God calls us
to have peace within our own hearts
and to live peacefully with those around us?

Peace is more important than all justice; and **peace** was not made for the sake of *justice*, but *justice* for the sake of **peace**.

MARTIN LUTHER

Use these two pages to portray a place
you can always go to feel peaceful.

As we pour
out our
bitterness
God pours
in his
peace.

F. B. MEYER

What signals does your body send when you
are becoming overwhelmed and stressed?
Write them down, then write ways
you can find peace in the midst of stress.

Do not be anxious about anything, but in everything by prayer and supplication with thanksgiving let your requests be made known to God. And the peace of God, which surpasses all understanding, will guard your hearts and your minds in Christ Jesus.

PHILIPPIANS 4:6-7

On this page, write down your biggest worries.
Then color over them with black marker.

On the next page, using a colorful pen or marker,
write three things that always make you feel peaceful.

Aim for restoration,
comfort one another,
agree with one another,
live in peace;
and the God of love
and peace will be
with you.

2 CORINTHIANS 13:11

Think of someone you've been in conflict
with or someone you've wronged.
How can you make amends and bring
peace to the relationship?

Our

peace shall stand

as firm

as rocky mountains.

WILLIAM SHAKESPEARE

13

On this page and the next,
describe or illustrate peace
as you would to a child.

There is

peace

even in
the storm.

VINCENT VAN GOGH
The Letters of Vincent van Gogh

DAY

14

The next time you are out in public, pause for a
moment to take in the environment around you.

Look at the people rushing about you.
Listen to the sounds and smell the air around you.

Focus on being present in that moment,
and with each breath imagine inhaling peace.
What did you notice that you wouldn't have
if you hadn't taken a moment to pause?

Peacemakers
who sow in
peace reap
a harvest of
righteousness.

JAMES 3:18, NIV

On these two pages, depict mundane activities
whose regularity and steadfastness bring you peace.

*Worry
does not empty
tomorrow
of its sorrows,
it empties today
of its strength.*

CORRIE
TEN BOOM

What are five ways you can let go of control today
and instead choose to take hold of peace?

If we have
no peace,
it is because
we have forgotten
that we belong
to each other.

MOTHER TERESA

DAY
17

Write and illustrate
your own poem about peace.

Consider the
blameless,
observe
the upright;
a future awaits
those who seek
peace.

PSALM 37:37, NIV

Reflect on a time recently
when you felt truly at peace.

In peace I will
lie down and sleep,
for you alone, LORD,
make me dwell
in safety.

PSALM 4:8, NIV

DAY
19

Depict peaceful scenes from nature
on these two pages.

Peace comes
when there is no cloud
between us and God.
Peace is the consequence
of forgiveness, God's removal
of that which obscures His
face and so breaks
union with Him.

CHARLES H. BRENT

DAY
20

If peace were a season,
would it be winter, spring, summer, or fall?
Illustrate or describe it.

God cannot *give* us
a happiness and peace
apart from *Himself,*
because it is not there.
There is no
such *thing.*

C. S.
LEWIS

On this page, describe something that is a source
of anxiety for you. On the next page, describe a way
God can bring you peace in the midst of your anxiety.

To make *peace*
with an *enemy*, one
must work *with*
that *enemy*, and
that enemy becomes
one's *partner*.

NELSON MANDELA

Think of a few ways you can bring peace
into situations of disagreement or anxiety
with your friends or family.

Blessed are the peacemakers, for they will be called children of God.

MATTHEW 5:9, NIV

Think of a song that always makes you
feel peaceful. Describe or illustrate images
that accompany your feelings.

Keep peace with yourself; then you will be able to bring peace to others. A peaceful man does more good than a learned man.

THOMAS À KEMPIS

What are three simple things you can do
to cling to peacefulness when you're
beginning to feel unsettled?

Lord,
make me an
instrument
of thy peace.

Where there
is hatred,
let me sow
love.

ST. FRANCIS
OF ASSISI

Write out and illustrate a quote or Bible
verse that communicates peace to you.

We must do our business faithfully; without trouble or disquiet, recalling our mind to God mildly, and with tranquility, as often as we find it wandering from Him.

BROTHER LAWRENCE

What is a truth that can always bring you peace?
Write it here and then write it on your foot or shoe.
Whenever you start to feel stressed or afraid,
set your feet on the ground and imagine
grounding yourself in that truth.

For to us a child is born,

to us a son is given;

and the government shall

be upon his shoulder,

and his name

shall be called

Wonderful Counselor,

Mighty God,

Everlasting Father,

Prince of Peace.

ISAIAH 9:6

Unpack a truth about God that has brought
you peace in a challenging season.

Peace
begins with a
smile.

MOTHER TERESA

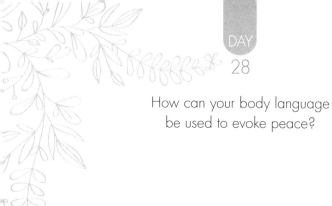

How can your body language
be used to evoke peace?

Deceit is in the heart of those who devise evil, but those who plan peace have joy.

PROVERBS 12:20

DAY

29

Use these two pages
to devise a plan for days when
peace is slipping from your grasp.

Peace
be with
you.

JOHN 20:21

How has your perception of peace
and your relationship with God
changed over the past thirty days?

But the fruit
of the Spirit is love,
joy, peace, patience,
kindness, goodness,
faithfulness,
gentleness,
self-control;
against such things
there is no law.

GALATIANS 5:22-23

Create Your Playlist

Create your own peaceful playlist here. You can either come to these pages each day to jot down a song that is speaking peace into your life that day or write down all at once your ideal playlist for adding peace to your life. Music has a unique way of activating our memory, so put together a playlist that will help you remember to choose peace each day and to remember the journey you took while writing in this journal. Once you've filled this out, we'd love to hear the playlist you came up with. Create your playlist on Spotify and share it with us by tweeting it to @WaterBrookPress and using #PlaylistPeace.

1 Song: _____
   Artist: _____

2 Song: _____
   Artist: _____

3 Song: _____
   Artist: _____

4 Song: _____
   Artist: _____

5 Song: _____
   Artist: _____

6 Song: _____
   Artist: _____

7 Song: _____
   Artist: _____

8 Song: _____
   Artist: _____

9 Song: _____
   Artist: _____

10 Song: _____
    Artist: _____

11 Song: _____
    Artist: _____

12 Song: _____
    Artist: _____

13 Song: _____
    Artist: _____

14 Song: _____
    Artist: _____

15 Song: _____
    Artist: _____

16 Song: _____
    Artist: _____

17 Song: _____
    Artist: _____

18 Song: _____
    Artist: _____

19 Song: _____
    Artist: _____

20 Song: _____
    Artist: _____

21 Song: _____
    Artist: _____

22 Song: _____
    Artist: _____

23 Song: _____
    Artist: _____

24 Song: _____
    Artist: _____

25 Song: _____
    Artist: _____

26 Song: _____
    Artist: _____

27 Song: _____
    Artist: _____

28 Song: _____
    Artist: _____

29 Song: _____
    Artist: _____

30 Song: _____
    Artist: _____

What I have learned about myself:

Where do I go from here?

About the Author

(Write your autobiography here.
Include your photograph, if you'd like.)

Acknowledgments

I would like to thank the following people
who have helped me discover peace:

Acknowledgments

The development team is grateful to all the individuals and departments within the Crown Division and WaterBrook for their help in creating this project, in particular Pam Fogle, Karen Sherry, and Julia Wallace.

Development Team

Kendall Davis

Jessica Lamb

Kristopher Orr

Sara Selkirk

Susan Tjaden

About the Illustrator

Laura Elizabeth Marshall is the owner of the Etsy shop DoodlingForDays, where she sells a variety of inspirational prints and designs. She has a heart for missions, and 100 percent of her Etsy proceeds go toward local and international mission work. Her talents include painting, design, and illustration, as well as custom chalkboard and calligraphy art. Laura is a first grade teacher and lives in Houston, Texas.

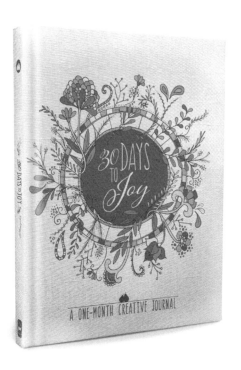

CREATE, DOODLE, WRITE, LAUGH, SING. THIS FUN
AND THOUGHTFUL JOURNAL TAKES YOU ON A MONTH-LONG
CREATIVE JOURNEY TO JOY.

See sample pages and more at WaterBrookMultnomah.com

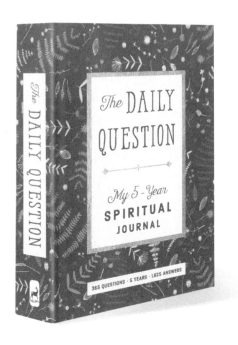

A THOUGHT-PROVOKING, 365-QUESTION GUIDED JOURNAL
THAT SPARKS DAILY REFLECTION ON FAITH AND
LIFE OVER A FIVE-YEAR PERIOD.

See sample pages and more at WaterBrookMultnomah.com

WATERBROOK